UKULELE

Disney® FUN SONGS

T0088555

ISBN 978-1-5400-4936-0

The following songs are the property of:

Bourne Co.
Music Publishers
5 West 37th Street
New York, NY 10018

I'VE GOT NO STRINGS
WHEN I SEE AN ELEPHANT FLY
WHISTLE WHILE YOU WORK
WHO'S AFRAID OF THE BIG BAD WOLF?

Visit Hal Leonard Online at
www.halleonard.com

Contact us:
Hal Leonard
7777 West Bluemound Road
Milwaukee, WI 53213
Email: info@halleonard.com

In Europe, contact:
Hal Leonard Europe Limited
42 Wigmore Street
Marylebone, London, W1U 2RN
Email: info@halleonardeurope.com

In Australia, contact:
Hal Leonard Australia Pty. Ltd.
4 Lentara Court
Cheltenham, Victoria, 3192 Australia
Email: info@halleonard.com.au

CONTENTS

*Based on the "Winnie the Pooh" works,
by A. A. Milne and E. H. Shepard

The Bare Necessities

from THE JUNGLE BOOK
Words and Music by Terry Gilkyson

Be Our Guest

from BEAUTY AND THE BEAST
Music by Alan Menken
Lyrics by Howard Ashman

Slightly faster

G   Gmaj7   G6   G

sing! They can dance! Af-ter all, Miss, this is France, ___ and a din-ner here is

G7   C6   B7

nev-er sec-ond best. Go on, un-fold your men - u, take a glance, ___

Em   A7   Am7   D7   G

___ and then ___ you'll be our guest, oui, our guest, be our guest!

E♭7   B♭m7   E♭7

2. Beef ra -

Verse
Slightly faster

A♭ 3fr

gout! Cheese souf - flé! Pie and pud - ding au flam - bé! We'll pre -

7

pare and serve with flair a cul-i-nar-y cab-a-ret! You're a-

lone and you're scared, but the ban-quet's all pre-pared. No one's

gloom-y or com-plain-ing while the flat-ware's en-ter-tain-ing. We tell

CHORUS:

jokes! I do tricks with my fel-low can-dle-sticks! And it's

LUMIÈRE:

all in per-fect taste: ____ that you can bet! Come on and

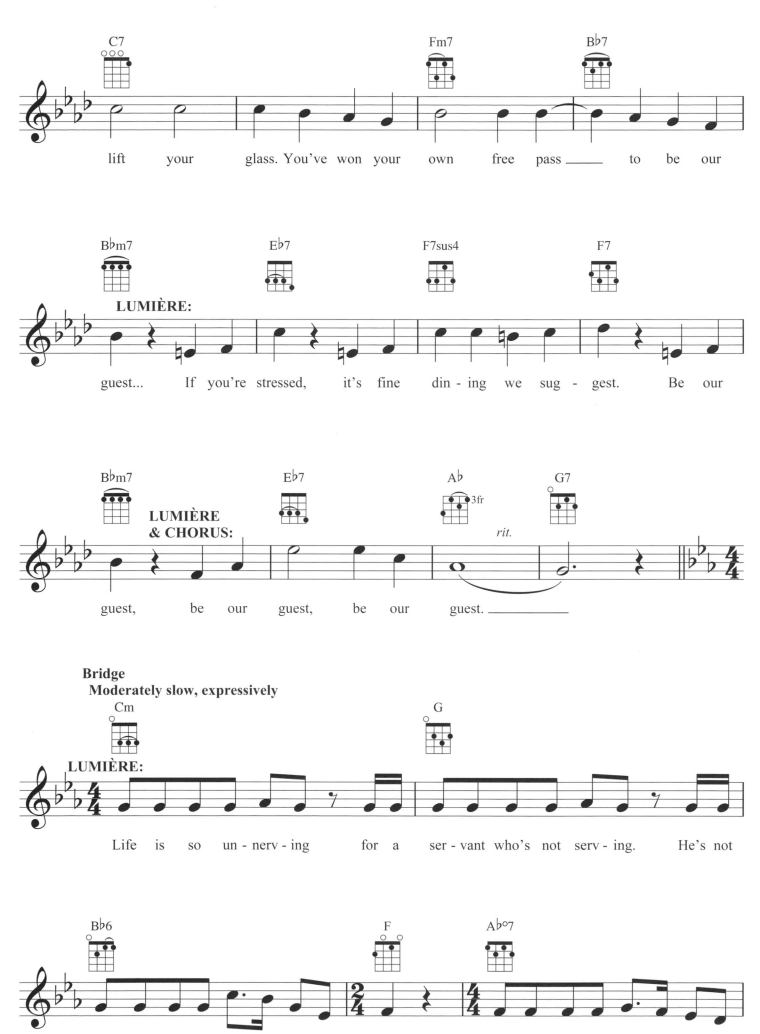

lift your glass. You've won your own free pass _____ to be our

LUMIÈRE:
guest... If you're stressed, it's fine din - ing we sug - gest. Be our

LUMIÈRE & CHORUS:
guest, be our guest, be our guest. _____

Bridge
Moderately slow, expressively

LUMIÈRE:
Life is so un - nerv - ing for a ser - vant who's not serv - ing. He's not

whole with - out a soul to wait up - on. Ah, those good old days when we were

use - ful, *(Spoken:)* eh, Cogsworth? Sud - den - ly those good old days are

gone. Too long we've been rust - ing, need - ing so much more than dust - ing: need - ing

ex - er - cise, a chance to use our skills!

Moderately fast, in 2

Most days we just lay a - round the cas - tle, flab - by, fat and la - zy. You walked

Verse

MRS. POTTS:

in, and oops - a - dai - sy! 3. It's a guest! It's a guest! Sakes a -

pressed. We've got a lot to do. Is it one lump, or two? For you, our guest. (She's our guest.) She's our guest. (She's our guest.) 4. Be our guest! Be our guest! Our command is your request. It's been years since we've had anybody here, and we're obsessed: With your meal, with your here, and we're obsessed: With your meal, with your

ease,   yes, in - deed   we aim to please.

While the   can - dle - light's still   glow   -   ing,

let   us   help   you. We'll keep   go   -   ing.

Outro-Verse
Slowly

Course   by   course,   one   by

gradually faster   **Moderately fast, in 2**

one,   'til you shout, "E- nough! I'm   done!" Then we'll sing you off   to

sleep as you di - gest. To - night you'll prop your feet ___

___ up, but for now let's eat ___ up. Be our guest!

Be our guest! Be our guest! Please

be our guest! ___

Friend Like Me

from ALADDIN

Music by Alan Menken
Lyrics by Howard Ashman

Bridge 2

ab - ra - ca - da - bra, let 'er rip and then make the suck - er dis - ap - pear?

D.S. al Coda

Coda

2. So don't - cha had a friend, you ain't

nev - er had a friend, nev - er had a friend, you ain't nev - er

Outro

had a _____ friend like me. _____

_____ Wa - ah - ah. Wa - ah - ah.

You ain't nev - er had a friend like me. _____ Ha!

Bibbidi-Bobbidi-Boo
(The Magic Song)

from CINDERELLA
Words by Jerry Livingston
Music by Mack David and Al Hoffman

Ev'rybody Wants to Be a Cat

from THE ARISTOCATS
Words by Floyd Huddleston
Music by Al Rinker

time he plays! ___ But with a square in the act, ___ you can

set mu - sic back ___ to the cave - man days! ___   2. I've

Verse

heard some corn - y birds who tried to sing,   but still a

3. Ev - 'ry - bod - y wants to be a cat,   be - cause a

cat's the on - ly cat who knows how to swing! ___   Who

cat's the on - ly cat who knows where it's at! _____   When

wants to dig a long - haired gig and stuff like that, _____

play - ing jazz you al - ways has a wel - come mat, _____

when ev - 'ry - bod - y wants to be a cat? ___   A

'cause ev - 'ry - bod - y digs a swing - ing cat! ___

Hawaiian Roller Coaster Ride

from LILO & STITCH

Words and Music by Alan Silvestri and Mark Keali'i Ho'omalu

There's no ___ place I'd rath-er be than on my surf-board out at sea.
There's no ___ place I'd rath-er be than on the sea-shore dry, wet, free.

Lin-ger-ing ___ in the o-cean blue. And if I had one wish come true, I'd
On gold-en ___ sand is where I'd lay, and if I on-ly had my way, I'd

surf 'til ___ the sun sets ___ be - yond the ___ ho - ri - zon.
play 'til ___ the sun sets ___ be - yond the ___ ho - ri - zon.

A - wi - ki - wi - ki, mai ___ lo hi lo hi. La - we mai i ko pa - pa he'e na-lu.
La - la - la i ka la ha - na-ha - na. Me ke kai ho - en e i ka pu'e o - ne.

Let's get jump-in', surf's _ up and pump-in'. Coast-in' with the mo - tion of the o - cean.

N.C.

D.C. al Coda
(Lyric 1)

Whirl-pools swirl - ing, cas - cad - ing, twirl - ing. Ha - wai - ian roll - er coast - er ride.

Coda

La - la - la i ka la ha - na - ha - na. Me ke kai ho - en - e i ka pu'e o - ne.

He - le - he - le mai ka - kou e. Ha - wai - ian roll - er coast - er ride.

Hakuna Matata

from THE LION KING
Music by Elton John
Lyrics by Tim Rice

ta - ta. _____ Why, when he was a young wart -

hog... _____ *P:* When I was a young wart - hog! *T: Very nice. P: Thanks. T: He*

found his a - ro - ma lacked a cer - tain ap - peal. __ He could clear the sa - van - nah af - ter

ev - 'ry meal! __ *P:* I'm a sen - si - tive soul, though I seem thick -

skinned. And it hurt that my friends nev - er stood down -

wind! And, oh, _____ the shame! He was a -

shamed! Thought of chang-in' my name! Oh, what's in a name? And I got down-

heart - ed... How did you feel? ___ ...ev -'ry time that I... *T: Hey, Pumbaa, not in front of the kids.*

Chorus

P: Oh, sorry. *Both:* Ha - ku - na Ma - ta - ta...

what a won - der - ful phrase. Ha - ku - na Ma -

ta - ta... ain't no pass - ing craze.

Simba: It means no wor - ries for the rest ___ of your days. ___

T. & S.: It's our prob - lem - free _____

_____ P: phi - los - o - phy. _____ T. & S.: Ha - ku - na Ma -

Bridge

ta - ta. _____ All: Ha - ku - na Ma - ta - ta. Ha -

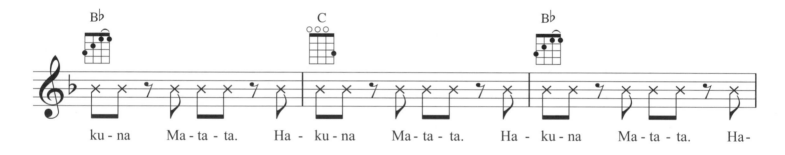

ku - na Ma - ta - ta. Ha - ku - na Ma - ta - ta. Ha -

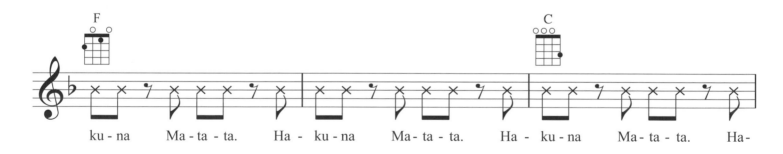

ku - na Ma - ta - ta. Ha - ku - na Ma - ta - ta. Ha -

T: ku - na... It means no wor - ries _____ for the rest ___ of your days. _

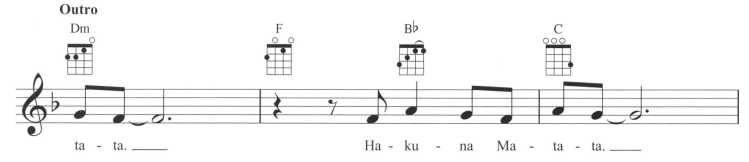

I Just Can't Wait to Be King

from THE LION KING
Music by Elton John
Lyrics by Tim Rice

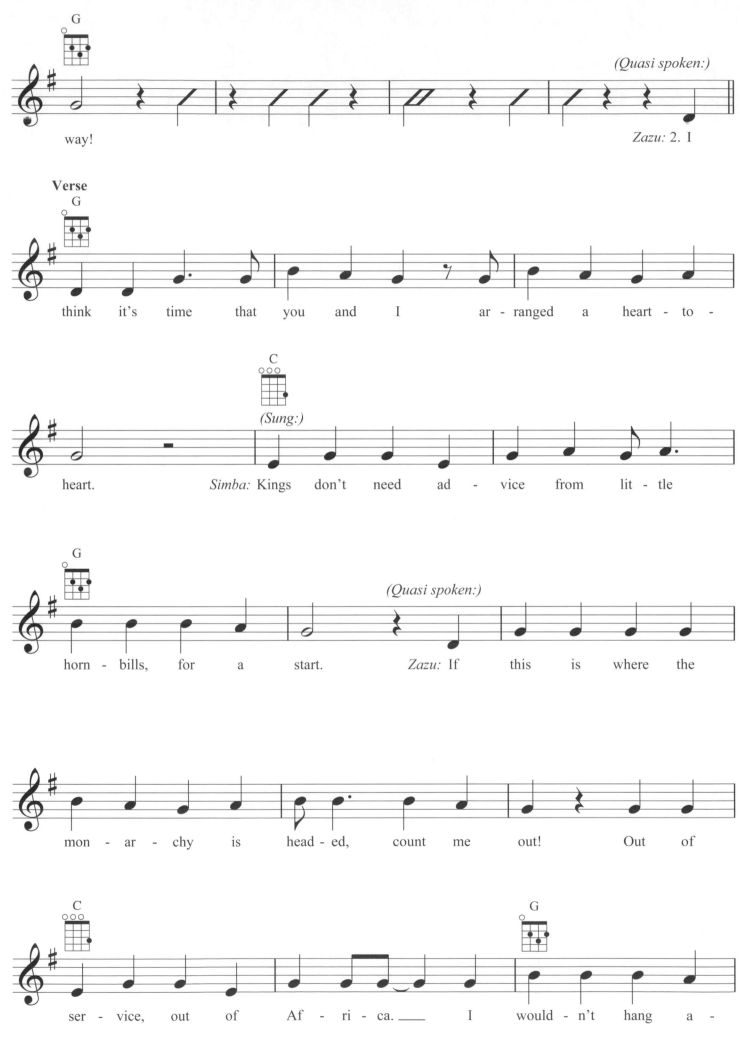

way!

(Quasi spoken:)

Zazu: 2. I

Verse

think it's time that you and I ar - ranged a heart - to -

(Sung:)

heart. *Simba:* Kings don't need ad - vice from lit - tle

(Quasi spoken:)

horn - bills, for a start. *Zazu:* If this is where the

mon - ar - chy is head - ed, count me out! Out of

ser - vice, out of Af - ri - ca. ___ I would - n't hang a -

hear it in the herd and on ___ the wing. _____ It's

gon - na be King Sim - ba's fin - est fling. *Simba:* Oh, I

just can't ___ wait to be king. Oh, I

just can't ___ wait to be king. Oh, I

Outro

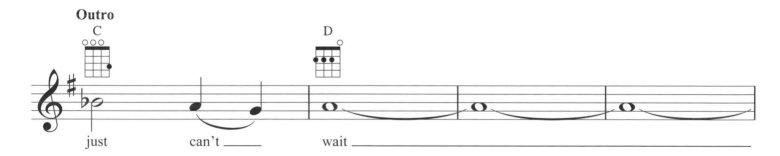

just can't ___ wait _____

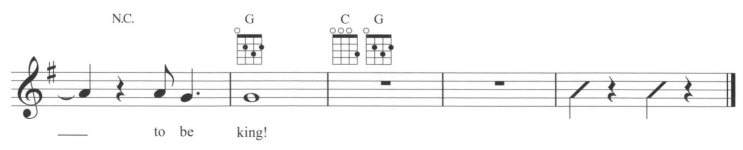

___ to be king!

I've Got No Strings

from PINOCCHIO
Words by Ned Washington
Music by Leigh Harline

If I Didn't Have You

from MONSTERS, INC.

Music and Lyrics by Randy Newman

Sulley: 1. If I were a rich man with a mil-lion or two

Mike: I'd live in a pent - house in a room with a view.

Sulley: And if I were hand - some, (It could happen.)

Mike: No way!

Sulley: 'cause dreams do come true,

I would-n't have noth-in' if I did-n't have you. Would-n't have

noth-in' if I did-n't have, __ would-n't have noth-in' if I did-n't have, __

Verse

would-n't have noth-in'. *Mike:* 2. For years I have en-

Mike: Can I tell you something?

- vied your grace and your charm. __

Sulley: You're green with it.

Ev-'ry-one loves __ you, you know. __ *Sulley:* Yes, I

know, I know, __ I know. *Mike:* But I must ad-mit it,

Supercalifragilisticexpialidocious

from MARY POPPINS

Words and Music by Richard M. Sherman and Robert B. Sherman

First note

Chorus
Brightly, in 2

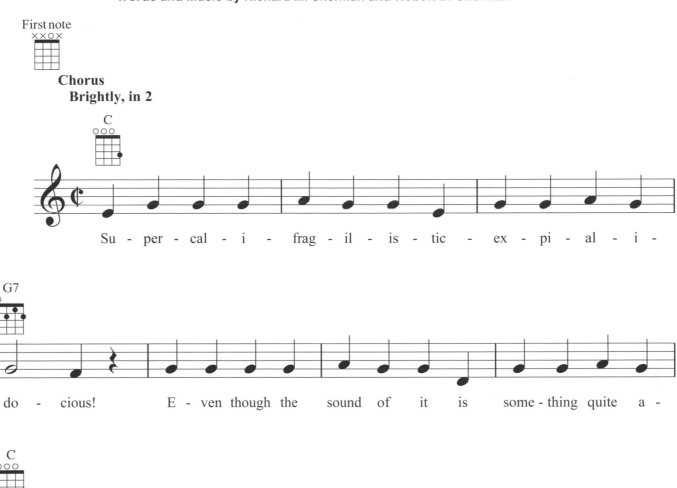

Su - per - cal - i - frag - il - is - tic - ex - pi - al - i -

do - cious! E - ven though the sound of it is some - thing quite a -

tro - cious, if you say it loud e - nough, you'll

al - ways sound pre - co - cious. Su - per - cal - i -

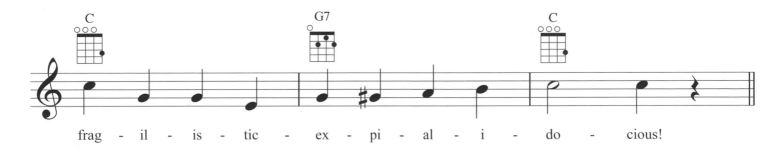

frag - il - is - tic - ex - pi - al - i - do - cious!

Interlude

Um did-dle did-dle did-dle, um did-dle ay! Um did-dle did-dle did-dle,

Verse

um did-dle ay!
1. Be - cause I was a - fraid to speak when
2. He trav - eled all a - round the world and
3. So when the cat has got your tongue, there's

I was just a lad, me fa - ther gave me
ev - 'ry - where he went he'd use his word and
no need for dis - may. Just sum - mon up this

nose a tweak and told me I was bad. But
all would say, "There goes a clev - er gent!" When
word and then you've got a lot to say. But

then one day I learned a word that saved me ach - in'
dukes and ma - 'a - ra - jas word pass the time of day with
bet - ter use it care - ful - ly or it can change your

nose, the big - gest word you ev - er 'eard and
me, I say me spe - cial word and then they
life. One night I said it to me girl and

44

this is 'ow it goes: Oh! (1.,2.) Su - per - cal - i -
ask me out to tea. Oh!
now me girl's me wife. She's (3.) Su - per - cal - i -

frag - il - is - tic - ex - pi - al - i - do - cious!
frag - il - is - tic - ex - pi - al - i - do - cious!

E - ven though the sound of it is some - thing quite a -
Su - per - cal - i - frag - il - is - tic - ex - pi - al - i -

tro - cious, if you say it loud e - nough, you'll
do - cious! Su - per - cal - i - frag - il - is - tic -

al - ways sound pre - co - cious. Su - per - cal - i -
ex - pi - al - i - do - cious! Su - per - cal - i -

1., 2.   3.

frag - il - is - tic - ex - pi - al - i - do - cious!
frag - il - is - tic - ex - pi - al - i - do - cious!

In Summer

from FROZEN

Music and Lyrics by Kristen Anderson-Lopez and Robert Lopez

First note

Verse
Easy Swing

OLAF: 1. Bees - 'll buzz; kids -'ll blow dan - de - li - on fuzz, and

I'll be do - ing what - ev - er snow does in sum - mer. _____

A drink in my hand, my

snow up a - gainst the burn - ing sand, __ prob - 'ly get - ting gor - geous - ly tanned in

Bridge

sum - mer. _____ I'll fi - n'lly see a sum - mer breeze _ blow a -

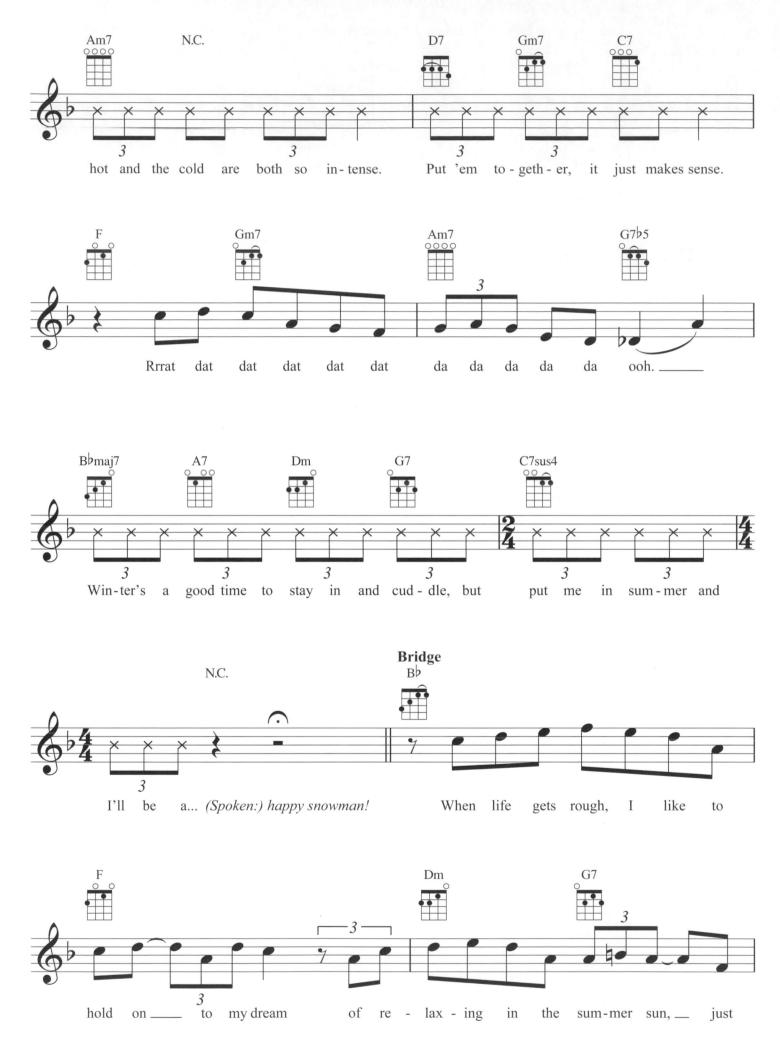

hot and the cold are both so in-tense. Put 'em to-geth-er, it just makes sense.

Rrrat dat dat dat dat dat da da da da da ooh. ____

Win-ter's a good time to stay in and cud-dle, but put me in sum-mer and

Bridge

I'll be a... *(Spoken:)* happy snowman! When life gets rough, I like to

hold on ____ to my dream of re-lax-ing in the sum-mer sun, ___ just

let - tin' off steam. ___   3. Oh, the

Verse

sky ___ will be blue,   and   you guys - 'll be there too...   when I

fi - nal - ly do what fro - zen things do in sum - mer. _____

Outro

N.C.

KRISTOFF: *(Spoken:) I'm gonna tell him.*   **ANNA:** *Don't you dare!*   **OLAF:** In

sum - mer! _____

Lava

from LAVA

Music and Lyrics by James Ford Murphy

Male: 1. A long, long time a - go, there was a volcano living all a - lone in the middle of the sea. He sat high a - bove his bay, watching all the couples play and wishing that he had some - one, too.

2. But little did he know that, living in the sea below, another volcano was listening to his song. Ev'ry day she heard his tune, her lava grew and grew, because she believed his song was meant for her.

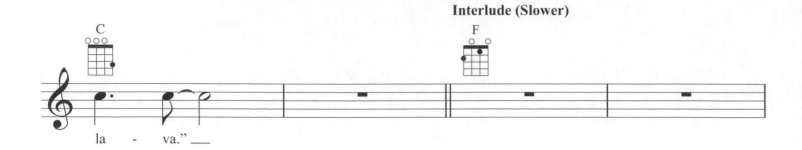

Interlude (Slower)

la - va." ___

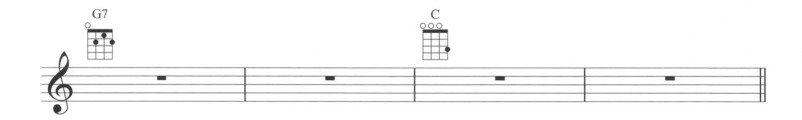

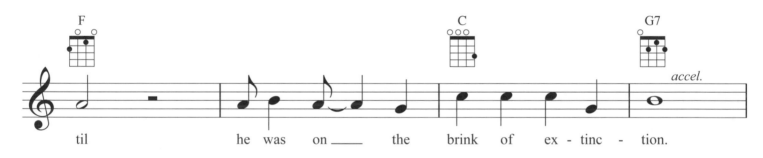

Verse

2. Years of sing - ing all a - lone ___ turned his la - va in - to stone ___ un -

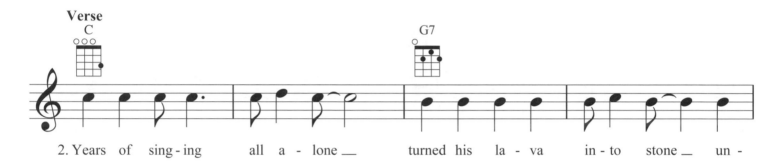

til he was on ___ the brink of ex - tinc - tion.

accel.

D.C. al Coda

CODA

rit. **Tempo I**

la - va." ___

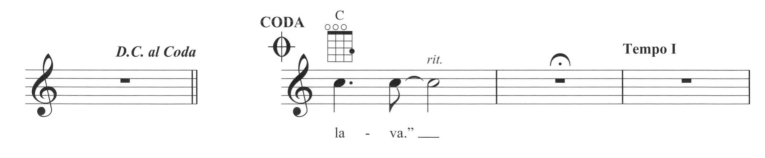

Verse

3. Ris - ing from the sea be - low ___ stood a love - ly

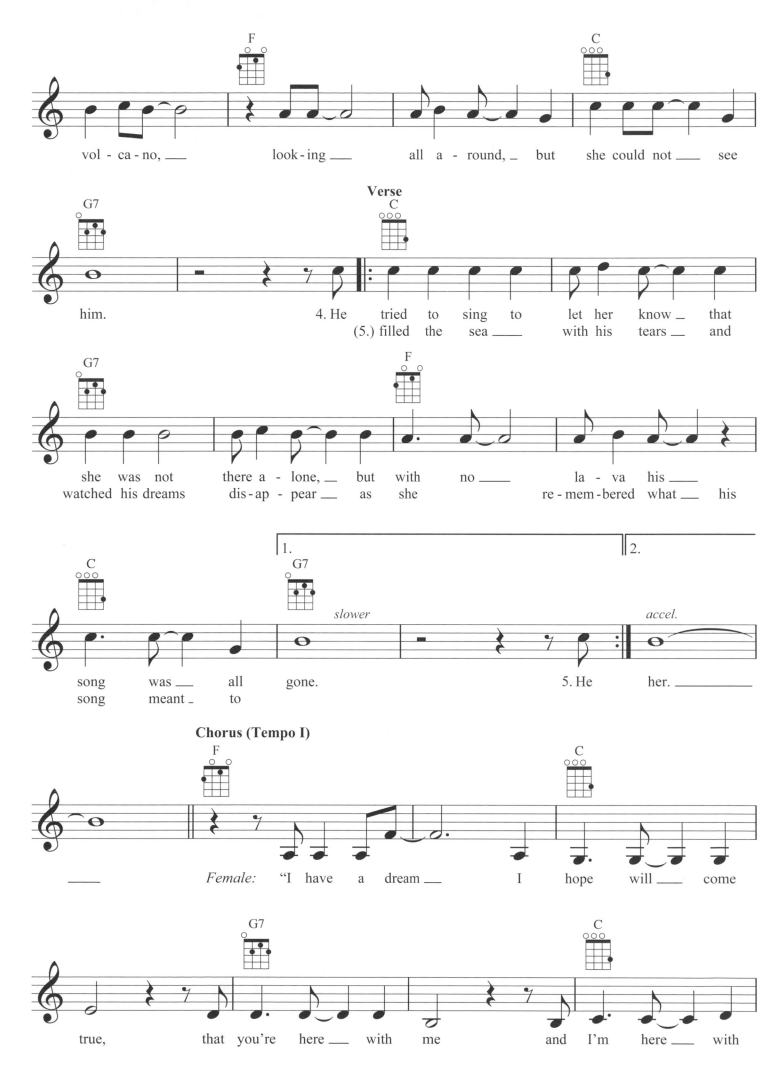

vol - ca - no, ___ look - ing ___ all a - round, ___ but she could not ___ see

Verse

him. 4. He tried to sing to let her know ___ that
(5.) filled the sea ___ with his tears ___ and

she was not there a - lone, ___ but with no ___ la - va his ___
watched his dreams dis - ap - pear ___ as she re - mem - bered what ___ his

1. *slower* 2. *accel.*

song was ___ all gone. 5. He her. ___
song meant ___ to

Chorus (Tempo I)

___ *Female:* "I have a dream ___ I hope will ___ come

true, that you're here ___ with me and I'm here ___ with

you. I ____ wish that ____ the earth, sea ____ and the sky up ____ a -

bove - a will send me some - one to la - va." ____

Interlude

a tempo

Verse

Male: 6. Oh, they were so hap - py ____ to fi - n'lly meet a -
(7.) long - er are they all a - lone, ____ with *a - lo - ha* ____ as

bove the sea. ____ All ____ to - geth - er now ____ their
their new home, ____ and when you vis - it them ____

1.

2.

la - va grew and grew. 7. No
this is what they sing.

Chorus

Both: "I have a dream ___ I hope will ___ come

true,   *Male:* (Ooh.) ___   and   I'll grow old   with you. ___
Female: that   you'll grow old   with me, ___   (Ah.) ___

___   *Both:* We   thank ___ the   earth,   sea, ___ and the   sky   we ___ thank, ___

too.   I   la   -   va   you.

I   la   -   va   you. ___

rit.   I   la   -   va   you." ___

One Jump Ahead

from ALADDIN
Music by Alan Menken
Lyrics by Tim Rice

that's no joke. ___ / head of the flock. ___

These guys / I think I'll

don't ap - pre - ci - ate I'm / take a stroll a - round the

Bridge

broke. / block.

Crowd: Riff raff! ___ / *Crowd:* Stop, thief! ___

Street rat! ___ / Van - dal! ___

Scoun - drel! ___ / Out - rage! ___

Take that! ___ / Scan - dal! ___

Aladdin: Just a _____ / *Aladdin:* Let's not ___

lit - tle ___ / be too ___

snack, guys. _____ / hast - y. _____

Crowd: Rip him o - pen, take it / *Lady:* Still, I think he's rath - er

back, guys. *Aladdin:* I can take a hint, got - ta face the facts. / tast - y. *Aladdin:* Got - ta eat to live, got - ta steal to eat.

One jump a - head of the hoof - beats, one hop a - head of the hump. ___ One trick a - head of dis - as - ter. They're quick, but I'm much fast - er. Here goes. Bet - ter throw my hand in. Wish ___ me hap - py land - in'. All ___ I got - ta do is jump!

A Spoonful of Sugar

from MARY POPPINS

Words and Music by Richard M. Sherman and Robert B. Sherman

cake. A lark! A spree! It's
toot. He knows A spree! It's
sip. And hence, they song will
     they find their

Chorus

ver - y clear to see that a
move the job a - long. For a spoon - ful of
task is not a grind. For a

sug - ar helps the med - i - cine go down, the med - i - cine go

dow - wown, med - i - cine go down. Just a spoon - ful of

sug - ar helps the med - i - cine go down in a most de -

1., 2.

light - ful way. 2. A rob - in way.
                3. The hon - ey -

3.

Un Poco Loco

from COCO
Music by Germaine Franco
Lyrics by Adrian Molina

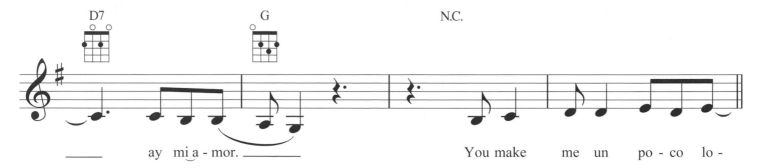

ay mi a - mor. ____ You make me un po - co lo -

Chorus 1

- co, ____ un po - qui - ti - ti - to lo - co. ____ The

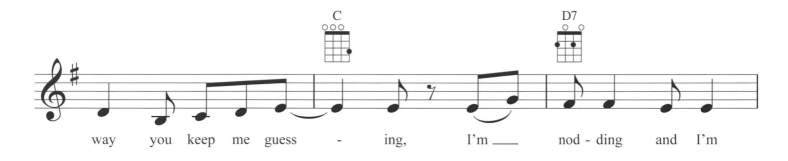

way you keep me guess - ing, I'm ____ nod - ding and I'm

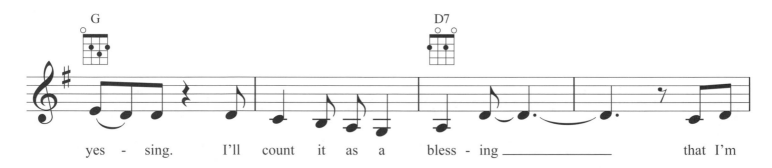

yes - sing. I'll count it as a bless - ing _____ that I'm

on - ly un po - co lo - co. _____

Interlude

Play 6 times

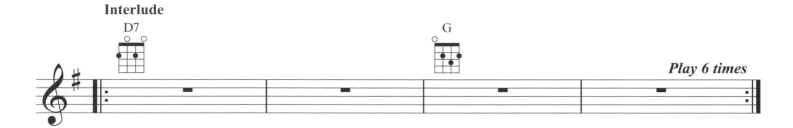

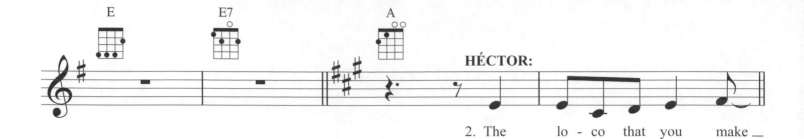

2. The lo - co that you make __

Verse

__ me, it is just un __ po - co cra - zy. __ The

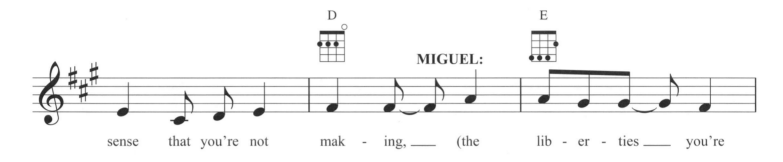

sense that you're not mak - ing, __ (the lib - er - ties __ you're

tak - ing,) __ leaves my ca - be - za shak - ing. __

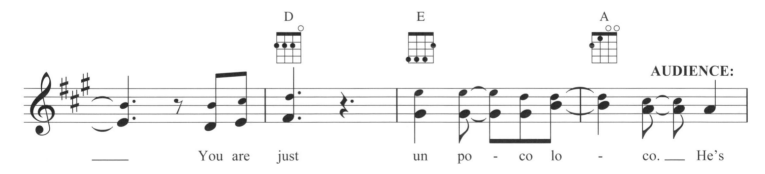

__ You are just un po - co lo - co. __ He's

Chorus 2

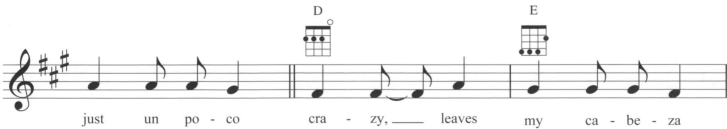

just un po - co cra - zy, __ leaves my ca - be - za

shak - ing. ___ He's just un po - co cra - zy, ___ leaves my ca - be - za

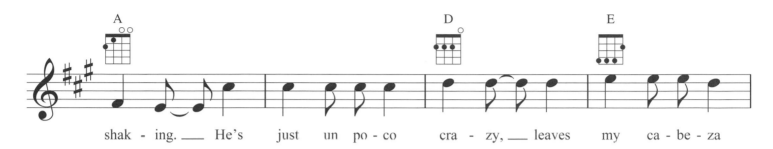

shak - ing. ___ He's just un po - co cra - zy, ___ leaves my ca - be - za

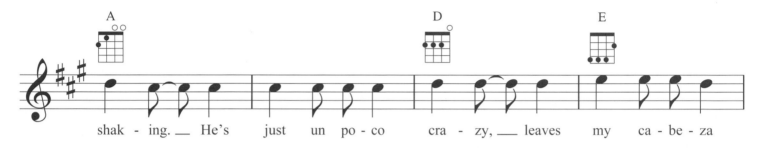

shak - ing. He's just un po - co cra - zy, ___ leaves my ca - be - za

Outro

shak - ing. ___ **HÉCTOR:** (Un po - qui - ti - ti - ti - ti - ti - ti - ti -
MIGUEL: Un po - qui - ti - ti - ti - ti - ti - ti - ti -

ti - ti - ti - ti - ti - ti - ti - ti - ti - ti - ti - to lo - co.) ___
ti - ti - ti - ti - ti - ti - ti - ti - ti - to lo - co. ___

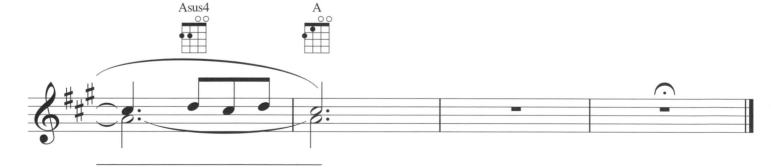

The Unbirthday Song

from ALICE IN WONDERLAND
Words and Music by Mack David, Al Hoffman and Jerry Livingston

First note

Verse
Moderately bright, in 2

Sta - tis - tics prove, prove that you've one

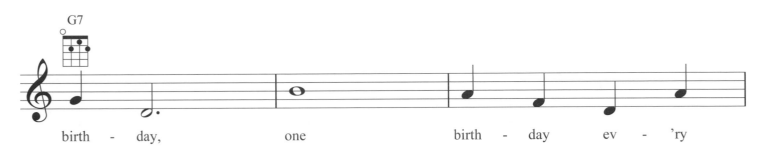

birth - day, one birth - day ev - 'ry

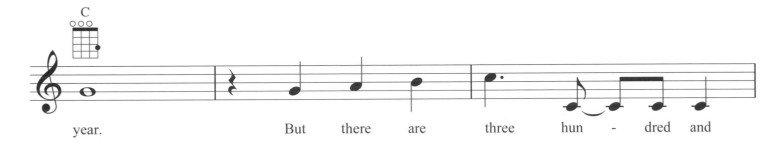

year. But there are three hun - dred and

six - ty - four un - birth - days; that is why we're

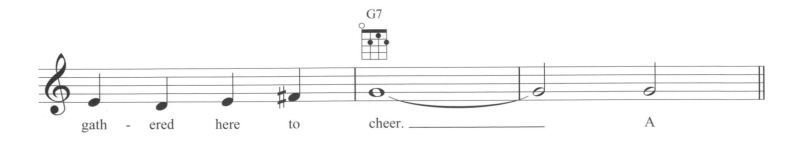

gath - ered here to cheer. _____ A

Under the Sea

from THE LITTLE MERMAID
Music by Alan Menken
Lyrics by Howard Ashman

Bridge

_____ play the flute. The carp _____ play the harp. The plaice _____ play the bass, and they _____

_____ sound - in' sharp. The bass _____ play the brass. The chub _____ play the tub. The fluke _____

_____ is the duke of soul. The ray, _____ he can play. The ling's _____

_____ on the strings. The trout _____ rock - in' out. The black - fish, she sings. The smelt _____

_____ and the sprat, they know _____ where it's at. And, oh, that blow - fish

Interlude

blow.

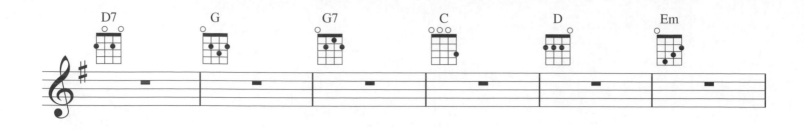

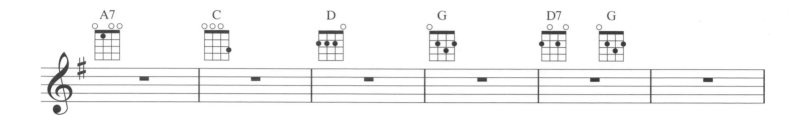

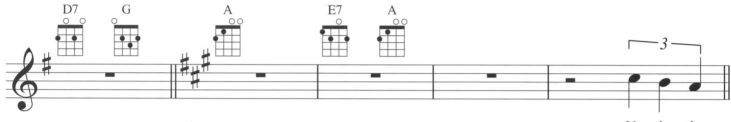

Un - der the

Chorus

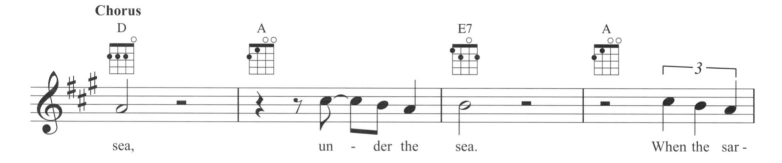

sea,   un - der the sea.   When the sar -

dine be - gin ___ the be - guine, it's mu - sic to me.

What do they got? A lot ___ of sand.   We got a

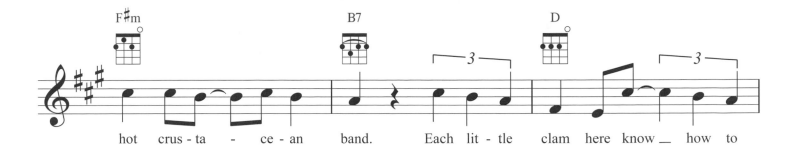

hot crus - ta - ce - an band. Each lit - tle clam here know __ how to

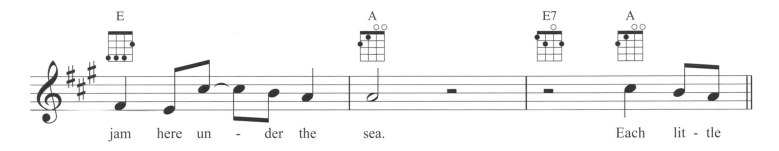

jam here un - der the sea. Each lit - tle

Outro

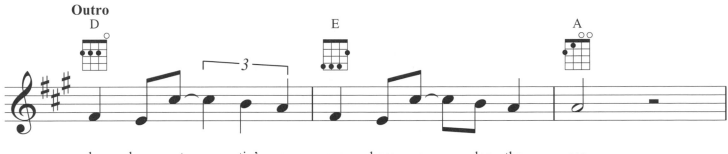

slug here cut - tin' a rug here un - der the sea.

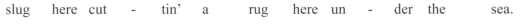

Each lit - tle snail here know __ how to wail here. That's __ why it's

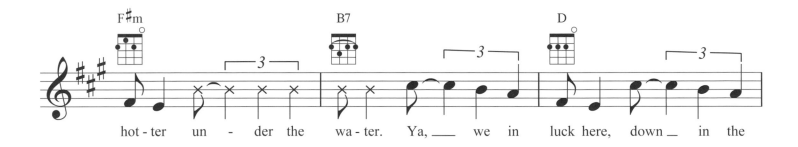

hot - ter un - der the wa - ter. Ya, __ we in luck here, down __ in the

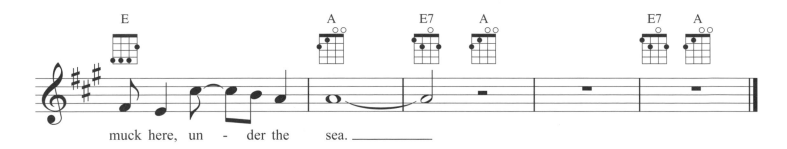

muck here, un - der the sea. _____

Whistle While You Work

from SNOW WHITE AND THE SEVEN DWARFS
Words by Larry Morey
Music by Frank Churchill

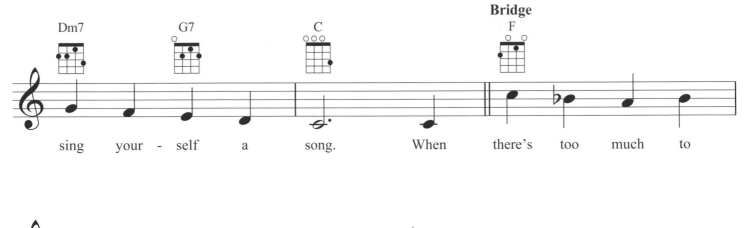

sing your - self a song. When there's too much to

do, don't let it both - er you. For -

get your trou - ble, try to be just like the cheer - ful

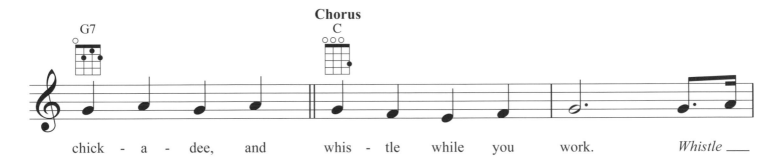

chick - a - dee, and whis - tle while you work. *Whistle* ___

___ Come on, get smart, tune

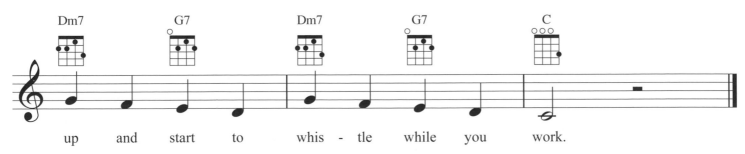

up and start to whis - tle while you work.

Who's Afraid of the Big Bad Wolf?

from THREE LITTLE PIGS
Words and Music by Frank Churchill
Additional Lyric by Ann Ronell

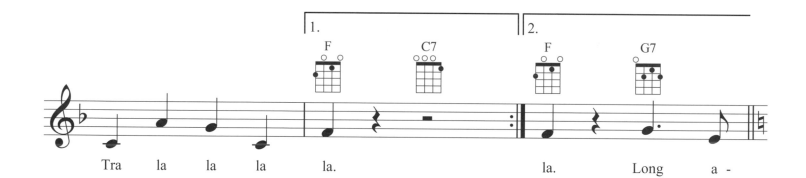

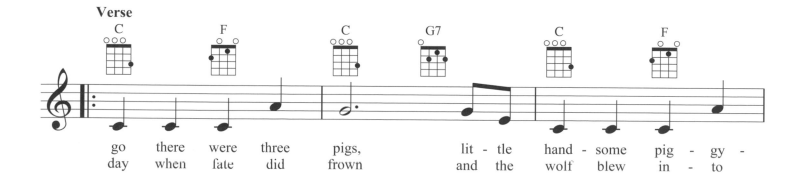

Pre-Chorus

The Wonderful Thing About Tiggers

from THE MANY ADVENTURES OF WINNIE THE POOH
Words and Music by Richard M. Sherman and Robert B. Sherman

Fun! But the most won-der-ful thing a-bout tig-gers is

To Coda

1.
I'm the on-ly one! 2. Oh, the one!

2.

Bridge

Tig-gers are cud-dl-y fel-las. _____ Tig-gers are aw-ful-ly

sweet. Ev-'ry-one el-es is jeal-ous. _____

D.S. al Coda

That's why I re-peat and re-peat: 3. The

Coda

one!

Yo Ho
(A Pirate's Life for Me)

from Disney Parks' Pirates of the Caribbean attraction

Words by Xavier Atencio
Music by George Bruns

You Can Fly! You Can Fly! You Can Fly!

from PETER PAN
Words by Sammy Cahn
Music by Sammy Fain

1. Think of a won-der-ful thought, an-y mer-ry lit-tle thought. Think of Christ-mas, think of snow, think of sleigh bells, here we go! Like rein-deer in the sky, ___ you can fly! You can fly! You can fly! ___
2. Think of the hap-pi-est things, that's the way to get your wings. Now you own a can-dy store. Look! You're ris-ing off the floor. Don't won-der how or why, ___ you can fly! You can
3. When there's a smile in your heart, there's no bet-ter time to start. It's a ver-y sim-ple plan. You can do what bird-ies can; at least it's worth a try, ___ you can

You're Welcome

from MOANA
Music and Lyrics by Lin-Manuel Miranda

First note

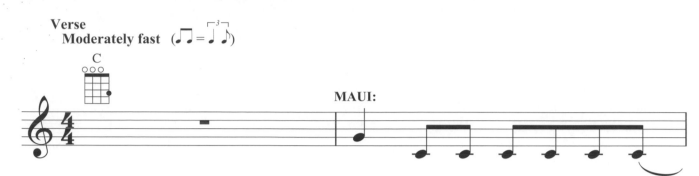

MAUI:

1. I see what's hap - pen - ing, yeah: ___

___ you're face to face with great - ness, and it's

strange. You don't e - ven know ___ how you feel. ___ It's a -

dor - a - ble. Well, it's nice to see that hu - mans nev - er

change. O - pen your eyes. ___ Let's ___ be - gin: ___ Yes, it's real - ly

me, it's Mau-i. Breathe it in, I know it's a lot: ___ the hair, ___ the bod, ___

___ when you're star-ing at a dem-i-god. ___ What can I say ___

Chorus

___ ex-cept, "You're wel - come, for the tides, ___ the sun, ___ the sky"? ___

___ Hey, it's o-kay, ___ it's o - kay: ___ you're wel - come. I'm

Verse

just an or-di-nar-y dem-i-guy. ___ 2. Hey, what has two thumbs ___

___ and pulled ___ up the sky ___ when you were wad-dl - ing

yea high? This guy! When the nights got cold, ____ who stole ____ you fire ____

____ from down be-low? You're look-ing at him, yo. Oh, al-so, I las-

-soed ____ the sun. ____ You're wel-come. ...To stretch your days and bring you fun. ____

____ Al-so, I har - nessed ____ the breeze. ____ You're wel-come. ...To

Chorus

fill your sails and shake your trees. ____ So what can I say ____

____ ex-cept, ____ "You're wel - come, for the is -

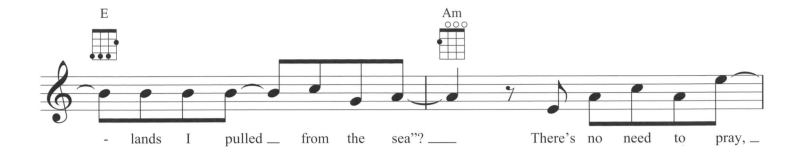

- lands I pulled _ from the sea"? ___ There's no need to pray, _

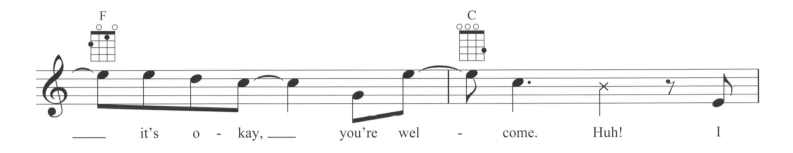

___ it's o - kay, ___ you're wel - come. Huh! I

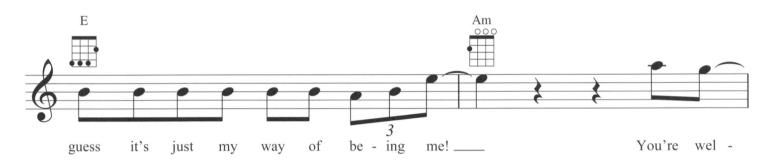

guess it's just my way of be - ing me! ___ You're wel -

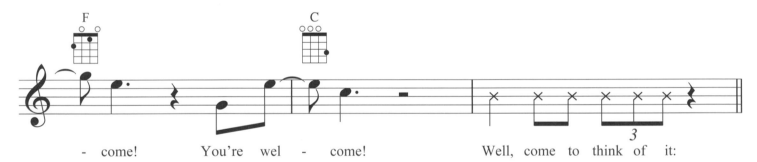

- come! You're wel - come! Well, come to think of it:

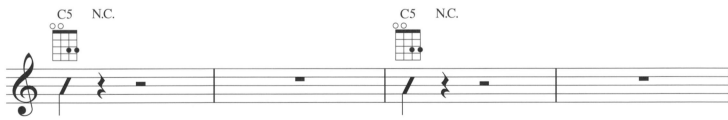

Rap: *(See additional lyrics)*

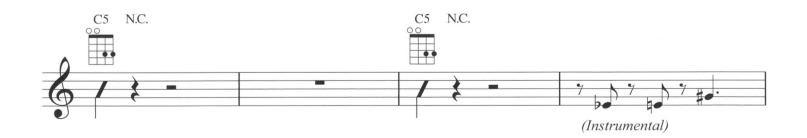

(Instrumental)

Outro-Chorus

(Rap ends) Well, an - y - way, ___ let me say, ___ "You're wel -

- come, for the won - der-ful world ___ you know." ___ Hey, it's o - kay, ___
(You're wel - come.)

___ it's o - kay: ___ you're wel - come. Well,
(You're wel - come.)

come to think of it, I got - ta go. ___ Hey, it's your day ___
(Ha, ha, ha.)

___ to say, ___ "You're wel - come," 'cause
(You're wel - come.)

Additional Lyrics

Rap: Kid, honestly, I could go on and on.
I could explain ev'ry nat'ral phenomenon.
The tide? The grass? The ground?
Oh, that was Maui, just messing around.

I killed an eel, I buried its guts,
Sprouted a tree: now you got coconuts!
What's the lesson? What is the takeaway?
Don't mess with Maui when he's on a breakaway.

And the tapestry here in my skin
Is a map of the vict'ries I win!
Look where I've been! I make ev'rything happen!
Look at that mean mini Maui, just tickety
Tappin'! Heh, heh, heh,
Heh, heh, heh, hey!

Zip-A-Dee-Doo-Dah

from SONG OF THE SOUTH
Words by Ray Gilbert
Music by Allie Wrubel

First note

Chorus
Merrily

G

Zip - a - dee - doo - dah,

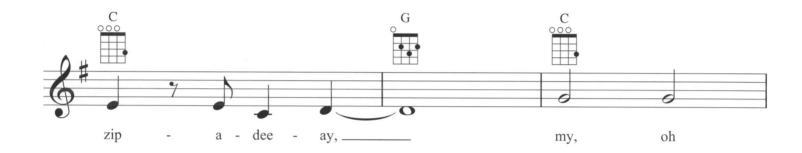

C   G   C

zip - a - dee - ay, _____ my, oh

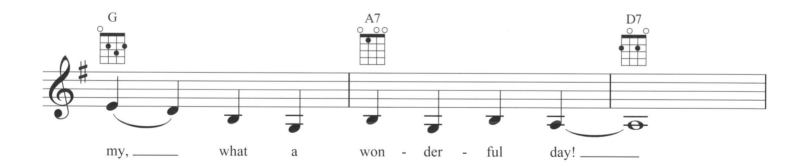

G   A7   D7

my, _____ what a won - der - ful day! _____

G   C

Plen - ty of sun - shine, head - in' my way, _____
Zip - a - dee - doo - dah, zip - a - dee - ay! _____

When I See an Elephant Fly

from DUMBO
Words by Ned Washington
Music by Oliver Wallace

polka-dot rail-road tie. But I think I will have seen
pick-et fence; that's __ no lie. But I think I will have seen

ev-'ry-thing __ when I see an el-e-phant fly.
ev-'ry-thing __ when I see an el-e-phant fly.

Bridge

I saw a clothes __ horse rar' up and buck. __ They
I e-ven heard __ a choc-o-late drop. __ I

tell me that a man made a veg-'ta-ble "Truck." __
went in-to a store, saw a bi-cy-cle shop. __

I did-n't see __ that, I on-ly heard, __ but
You can't de-ny __ the things that you see, __ but

just   to   be   so - cia - ble   I'll   take   their   word. ___   I   saw   a
I   know there's cer - tain things that   just   can't   be. ____   The   oth - er

Outro-Verse

lan - tern   slide, ____   saw   an   old   cow   hide, ___   and   I   just
day   by   chance, ___   saw   an   old   barn   dance, ___   so   I'm   a

laughed   till   I   thought ____   I'd   die.   But   I
gul - li - ble   sort _____   of   guy.   But   I

think   I   will   have   seen   ev - 'ry - thing ____   when
think   I   will   have   seen   ev - 'ry - thing ____   when

I   see   an   el - e - phant   fly.   2. I   saw   a
I   see   an   el - e - phant   fly.